This Book Belongs to

Personale information

Name:

Address:

Phone:

Social media:

Email:

Made in the USA
Monee, IL
24 May 2022

96980752R00069